Postcards
from the Lilac City

poems by

Mary Ellen Talley

Finishing Line Press
Georgetown, Kentucky

Postcards from the Lilac City

For My Parents
the real Fred and Ethel

ACKNOWLEDGMENTS

Chariton Review: "Blue Poem"
Flatbush Review: "The Poet's Coffin"
www.vietnamwarpoetry.com: "The Things We Carry"

Mary Ellen has been blessed with wonderful teachers at Seattle's Hugo House, including Judith Skillman, Carolyne Wright, and the late Judith Roche. Special thanks to Deborah Woodard for her teaching and support. Appreciation to the Greenwood Poets, founded by Sharon Cumberland, for years of weekly poetry feedback and to members of Women of a Certain Age poetry group. Thanks to Poets on the Coast headed by Kelli Russell Agodon and Susan Rich.

Grateful memories to my fifth-grade teacher mother who recited snippets of verse and bought home a small inscribed book of poetry to me when I was in the third grade. Gratitude to my husband Ken for sharing life and literary passions with me for fifty years and counting. Thank you to our visual artist son and daughter who balance out their bookish parents.

Publisher: Leah Maines
Editor: Christen Kincaid
Cover Art: Matthew Talley
Author Photo: Lifetouch Church Directories and Portraits, Inc.
Cover Design: Elizabeth Maines McCleavy

Order online: www.finishinglinepress.com
also available on amazon.com

Author inquiries and mail orders:
Finishing Line Press
P. O. Box 1626
Georgetown, Kentucky 40324
U. S. A.

Table of Contents

Because Once Upon a Time the God Pan
Was Smitten by the Wood Nymph Syrinx

In fear of Pan, she changed herself
into a reed. He could not bear to lose
the sweetest voice of all Arcadia,
so took a reed and crafted pan pipes
in her honor and her name.

Now knowing my late May common lilac,
syringa vulgaris, is of Eastern Europe's olive family,
I'm sure to drizzle extra virgin olive oil
over layers of sliced mozzarella, tomatoes,
and basil for my August caprese salad.

J.J. Browne planted two ornamental
lilac bushes in his Spokane yard in 1906,
one year before my mom was born
on a Trout Creek, Montana, homestead
where only essentials were planted.

John W. Duncan brought lilacs
from Rochester, NY, to Manito Park in 1912.
Spokane's Lilac Festival was born in 1938.
No parades during WWII years.
Syringa Spokane was introduced in 1999.

Since 1953, Lilac Princesses
have hailed from area high schools.
All the girls in town knew the parade wave:
elbow, elbow—wrist, wrist, wrist,
finger, finger—blow a kiss.

We waited, we wait
for those short weeks
when the entire city
can stand beside woody branches
to draw in the sweet purple scent.

Bike Riding Before Helmets

End of the Trolley Park

1.   Carousel at Natatorium Park, 1909-1967

Come back.
Watch families drawn to swimming,
baseball, gardens, rides, and cotton candy.
They picnic at the curve in the Spokane River,
not far from where two Chinese dragon benches
breathe fire. See the gilded carousel,
gift of master carver Charles Looff,
in honor of his daughter Emma's wedding.
One tiger, one giraffe, the benches,
and all of fifty-four painted horses
with bejeweled headpieces
gallop as the platform spins.
Revolving once,
each steed jumps six times.
Revolving twice,
my father leans right on the first date
in the Lilac City,
trying to catch the brass ring
with one outstretched hand.
                    It won't be a stylish marriage
                    I can't afford a carriage.
See now the end of an era,
five-cent trolley line gives way to cars and buses.
Merry-go-round and roller coaster
still stand another thirty years to host 4th of July fireworks
where we parked on the rise above for the best view.
Hush now.
The stallions are sleeping. Come.
Leave the slow descent to Nat Park.
The cemeteries are full
of riders.

2.   The Carousel Returns to Riverfront Park, 1975

Open crates in storage
and rouse each restless sleeper.
Wake up!
We will tend to your grooming,
sweep away years of dust, restore plumes,
re-glue each glass jewel. See how each sculpted giant
preens elegant shine in coats of paint and lacquer.
Come now. Enter the brick stable upriver,
where 333 mirrors revolve, and 180 lights
kaleidoscope color in the circular home.
Ticket takers welcome the parade of people
queuing up—now listening
to the organ's 300 hurdy-gurdy pipes.
Each animal glistens in waiting.
Throngs step to the wood plank platform
to take their pick—choose Red Sorrel,
Dapple Grey, Chocolate Pinto, Bay, or Palomino.
Stirrups ready for the climb aboard.
Grab the center pole, rise up,
throw a leg over and cinch the leather belt.
Organ music starts the slow circle
as the procession begins once again
with Oliver in the lead, head held high,
galloping forward.
               Gonna take a sentimental journey
as memories glisten spinning counterclockwise.
New generations tug the reins as steeds speed past
in hastening cadence.
Winded riders reach for the brass ring.

Let the trolleys sleep.

faith in the lilac city

now is
n't
maybe
whatever you suspected years ago

so the family on heroy street built a bomb shelter

filled with canned goods

all of you viewed as totally un
necessary

because everyone knew that the poor clare monastery

pro
tected the neighborhood

from any cold war bomb khrushchev might drop

do you
be
lieve

or laugh

at displays depicting assorted red & white dioramas

of ex
pired

camp
bell's soup cans on the shelves

As I Pursue You

1.
You joined hands with Mom every Memorial Day,
snipping buckets full

of lilacs and roses for the cemetery.
Standing on the ground, she bent over the porch

removing thorns
as if the dead might prick and bleed.

We laid a slight bouquet
for grandmas, grandpas, uncles,

and for Mickey of the fallen bicycle in Portland.
You paddled me when I was seven

for riding in the street. No reason
for another father to mourn his child.

2.
At age eleven, kitty-corner neighbor Kathy and I biked
through North Spokane streets on summer afternoons,

down Wellesley's long hill, past the V.A. Hospital
to enter an arch of stones, circa 1888,

then glide winding Fairmount Cemetery lanes
under the canopy of lofty pines.

We'd sit on cold monument steps and I'd tell
how you managed Uncle Frank's service station

while he was grieving Mickey in the City of Roses.
We'd peer at flowers in the locked stone chapels

of the richly dead, wave to the caretaker, ride home
past evergreen shadows shielding us from heat.

3.
Now I'm thirty-six, visiting you in cardiac recovery
where your anger jars me,

unaware what remnants pump through your bypass.
I wonder how I used to calm your tremoring hand

that sought relief in that third drink. Now I count
breaths while your lungs exhale mucous and debris.

I tell you of my toddler daughter perched on my bike,
realize that what I most recall is your steady hand

grasping the back of my bicycle
and you running beside me until I could not fall.

Duplex: We Had a Real Fred and Ethel in the Lilac City
(I Love Lucy was on CBS 1951-1967)

Fred and Ethel Mertz shot prime-time ridicule.
Lucy and Ricky Ricardo bantered lots.

Bantered lots in black 'n white TV we watched.
Weekly comic pratfalls and damn gender roles.

Damn gender roles they argued which was harder.
Swapped for burnt ironing and failure aprons.

Failure aprons as husbands ruined kitchens.
Wives wrapped chocolates on a job conveyor belt.

Conveyor belt raced by and wives got fired.
Our house with troubled Fred and Ethel chuckled.

They chuckled long past their own squabbles.
A little worse for wear their family downtime.

Family downtime watching comedy routines.
Swapped quarrels for shots of prime-time laugher.

Stone Man on Lilac Parade Float

Half-chiseled face
and firm-lipped visage
can't inhale the sweetness
amid symmetry
of a dozen virgin faces.
The quarry within him
stirs at the soft shoulders
he yearns to touch.
Fairest of the radiant ones
wears a crown
beside his marble torso.
His one eye roves
from a stern half face,
struggling to drink in the forms
so completely beguiling.
He would run up mountains
backwards
to inhale such scent
of damsels
before graduation
and departures
left him to imagine their deflowering.
Crowd stands on the bridge
not knowing that the stone man
would risk dismemberment
to take the fairest in descent
over Spokane Falls.
It is May and lilacs bloom
by mayoral proclamation.
Thousands of four-square buds
cup upward—flurry of tiny basket blossoms.
The stone man is close enough to catch their fragrance,
yet chaste enough
to protect maidens stepping down.

Butterfly

        I lift up the hood
of the rust-winged Impala
in the Holy Names High School parking lot,
proud to have my brother's discarded wheels—
        I, in my herringbone pleated skirt,
          blue anklets and white Peter Pan collar,
          history and French books tossed in the back seat.
Now to flip up the butterfly,
that metallic hinge
on top of the carburetor,
jump into the car
turn on the ignition
while my friends head to buses.
I let the car idle in *Park*—
        jump out
to tip the butterfly wing back down,
close the hood
while KJRB plays
Love Love Me Do, You Know I Love You,
and I anticipate the voice I'll hear after school,
Liverpudlian I met in August
at the Shadle Park slab dance on the tennis court
where the DJ spun 45s. We slow danced.

Now I hear Herman's Hermits
sing *Can't You Hear my Heartbeat*
as Liverpool and I rendezvous in the parking lot
under shade of an old lilac in the nearby park.
I'm free for an hour
until time to pick up
my fifth-grade teacher mom at Cooper Elementary.
She dozes as we head home to Walnut Street
our yard framed by brief lilacs and pink roses with thorns,
Impala parked in the driveway
all the butterfly wings closed for the night.

Spokane Postcards

Neighborhood Shop

We are mostly water,
and lick salt wounds, paper cuts,
potato chip factory dregs
five cent jam-packed bags on the corner
of Maple and Garland
in and out of lilac season.
Oil and thirst to last all week.

> *Dear Mom, I chose this train postcard for you,*
> *well, for obvious reasons. What a sorry excuse*
> *for an engine! Couldn't make it up the trestle-*
> *cable pull. It'll work for the suited rangers*
> *just past lumbermen who downed the ties.*
> *Your life depended on rails your dad, brothers,*
> *and my dad rolled across. Home soon. Love, ME*

Shadle Park

There are hours to kill.
Walk on the hill of wet grass
above the track. It tickles so good
after ten blocks of hot pavement.
Lie on night-cool grass without talking.
Kiss the space between his teeth.
Jackknife into flinging water
off the pool edge. Beaded wet,
I lie on a towel pulled from the bathroom.
Rough concrete. Scraped toes.
Sun-dried skin, jump back in.
Sandals flapping sidewalks,
pull petal soft sheer layers from burnt skin.
Drop it all on an ant hill.

Oh honey, we learned to ignore outhouse smells.
I just inhaled rows of corn or other incense grandpa tilled.
It was all we had left of Montana.
Lilacs bloom so briefly, we didn't plant any.
My hands were thick, the chickens eager.
Lord, the kitchen sweat, no matter how much powder
between my legs. Well, once I sat, I stayed.
Remember all the beans I snapped from the rocker
on the porch? Sorry if you inherited my knees.
Such pain, no worse for the chickens.
Love, Grandma

Gonzaga Prep

Bullpup blue
I roll my eyes
at the gridiron hero.
It seems the only reason
the guys invite me to dance
at the Friday night mixers
is to ask about my big brother.
I never sign my letters
Love X and kisses O.

*Dear Jim, This postcard. I'm the white wings, the sprite
standing lightly on a leaf of a lilac tree. You're an owl
on a firm branch ready to fly off to another football game.
I fried steak and eggs for you and your pals on game days
when mom was at work. Yet you gave me your belt and
told me to swing at the bees' nest to clear up my climbing
tree. The worst mom would do is call you a jackass as she
nursed my stings. By the time I hit high school you were
playing pro ball and had five children I adored. Love, ME*

Wandermere

Blue dot swimsuit, fanny ruffle.
Change in the cabana for a quarter.
North Spokane teens spend the day
at the Lilac City's man-made lake
past the first shopping mall in town.
Rainbow snow cone drips the chin.
Towel roll wet suit, prune skin.

> *Dear Rosie, There are curtains in the monastery*
> *windows and I am intensely curious to know if*
> *the monks ever sleep on the flat roofs. Remember playing*
> *with our dolls on the roof in summer? I never thought*
> *I'd get this far from home. Wouldn't the nuns be shocked*
> *to see a thousand Buddhist monks meditating.*
> *This place is 400 years old. I was given a white silk scarf*
> *of respect and I even tried yak butter. I am still so Spokane.*
> *I'm playing it safe, eating rice every day. Love, ME*

Walnut Street

Sun still shining. Dry heat.
Grasshoppers munch on dry grass
near the alley where rhubarb and lilacs
thrive beside the garbage can.
Turn the front sprinklers on
at night and sleep in the backyard.
Leave the back door open.
I didn't expect this card to be returned.

Dear Sylvia, Don't these medieval women remind you of nuns?
The one in green climbs the chicken coop, reaches for eggs.
Doesn't the braid of the lady in blue holding the bowl
look just like the one Rosie's mom fixed her every day?
See the balcony nun fending off chickens.
Could you see Sister Andrea Rose managing a crazy coop!
Note the pastel wash. I was thinking of you in Phoenix,
the hot sun and orange trees in your backyard. Call when
you're back in town. Love, ME

The Big Red Wagon

Photo op at Riverfront Park.
Now our grandkids slide down the handle,
visit Aunt Leslie
and drive her to the cemetery.
No one needs to buy lilacs in Spokane.
Such profusion
in a brief season.

Dear Mary, Sylvia, Kathy, Linda and the rest of us,
Fifty years since our graduation. We wore white gowns.
I was there with Ken. You didn't expect us to last.
The big city was Seattle. That's where we are now.
A few years back, I saw our old biology teacher climbing
Mt. Rainier. Sister Marian Sarto is no longer a nun.
Remember dissecting frogs in her class? Love, ME

Cheerleaders

Hot. Hot. So hot.
Nobody has to tell us twice
to wear thongs on our feet.
Kick-the-can in the street
and bike rides in summer.
Some girls aspire to be yell leaders
or Lilac Princesses
but they will have more options
because we'll subscribe
to *Ms.* magazine.

> *Dear Taylor and Aubrey, You have to come to Seattle
> for the bigger art exhibits. If you put enough colored dots
> on your floors and ceilings and tables and chairs like we
> did at the Yayoi Kusama exhibit, we'll all be counting
> using Aubrey's obstreperous method, while you kids are
> still doing slip jigs and riding bikes. Wish we could pick
> huckleberries together. Love, Grandma*

After Vietnam

The Things We Carry

I am reading a memoir of the war that incited our marriage.
Inside our lilac-scented city, you and I carried desire
like youth's cranking jump rope and I counted revolutions
while wearing those tan oxfords, tennies, or flip flops
we needed to protect our feet from Spokane's hot potato pavement.

Growing up near one another in a parallel universe,
not friends, but sometimes playing kick-the-can in Healy's spare lot—
I've forgotten the rules that have slid past open doors
of synapses tacked on telephone poles in our hometown.

I sip tea in our married house and open the book of war
someone must've watered down, or it would never be
on students' 10th grade reading list. Just now I turn the page
to sense the war that never stole you from me
after you commuted to college with Claudia, war widow next door.

Regretted folly to avoid the draft, you joined the Naval Reserve
but your lottery number was in the three hundreds, the flag-draped
coffin I had imagined with you inside would never come to pass.
Claudia lives in the same house and has buried her second husband.

Your Eastern diploma scored you typing memos for Seabees near LA
while low draft number grunts racked up PTSD and addictions
on jungle-shrouded mountains. I joined you. We newlyweds watched
medics calm a GI returnee near our apartment—writhing in flashback
for carnage he had seen, buddy who found a mine field with his foot.

Today we mail shamrock cookies to your mom, your sister,
our son, our flower girl and my sister whose husband survived duty
as a Medi-vac pilot in 'Nam but died early, in the end wielding
an oxygen tank, his pulmonary arterioles defoliated from Agent Orange.

I spread green frosting for the Irish month of our marriage.
The author tells readers that his text contains fact and fiction. In addition,

all is truth. Soldiers carried photos, pebbles in the mouth, a hatchet.
One wore his fiancé's nylons wrapped around his neck
and knew they brought him luck even after her Dear John letter.

Disheveled vets walk our city. Divorce courts spin romance
on a turntable. No pesticides for our yard, we dig up dandelion roots.
Our early union is an anecdote I add in telling teens of social history.
I tell them you survived, that we even drove to Vegas, and saw Elvis
in his prime.

Occupation of Lilacs

After Gertrude Stein

lavender is lavender cupped blossoms spreading cone-shaped green leaves soft full bush lavender lilac I stand near their fan inhale simple regalia on the steps of my porch Leo dead neighbor Leo dug up two lilac trees fifteen-years ago gave them away to bring spring smells beside our front porch I pause to breathe in fragrance on the steps without touching lean close almost touching brown tinge will come too soon impinge upon the edge of luminous lilac let it become brown burn die flower too soon keep now inhaling all the days of the bloom until breathing in loses the scent that stops me on the gray steps of my porch blossoms bending over the white railing I stop for one more perfect perfume I keep I keep inhaling

Hokey Pokey

Stand still for God's sake
until the camera flashes. No red eye
in the sepia stare space.
You put one roller skate in.
You put one roller skate out.
It's obvious you have to be steady
to hold hands in the big circle.
Two bucks per person Friday night
at Seattle's Bitter Lake Community Center
where families throng
roundabout the snack counter.
You hold hands with your mother
for the slow trek. Fast track
bites the dust and circle almost
unbroken. Hold on for dear life,
crack-the-whip skaters in a line
or you'll all end up purple.
One more time—look at the tilted cap. Let go!

You can bring the queen to tea by proxy
in the haze. Print the invitation
when the music at the rink changes
direction. Shake the expectation.
Your mom recalls her sixteenth birthday—
four girls at Spokane's Pattison's Rollercade
wearing sweatshirts inside out,
(style in the Lilac City) cropped sleeves,
cutoff jeans with nylons.
That's what it's all about.
You no longer hold the railing.
Skate backwards, eyes cast with the Mad Hatter,
weaving side to side—
waving across the varnished floor
until the deck of cards
falls down.

Heading Home from your Mother's Funeral

Drive past sagebrush
and crop signs on fences
along I-90,
recall times
your wife
pointed her finger
at the fifteen metal stallions,
Grandfather Cuts Loose the Ponies,
careening off Vantage hills
just before she led
seatbelt tethered
son and daughter
in arm motions—
Row, Row, Row Your Boat
across the Columbia.

Brash winds still
spread heat
at the public beach
where you stopped
for the kids to play,
picnicked on soda pop
and your mom's
Wonder Bread sandwiches,
sat on the grass
shaded by windswept trees
as children molded turrets
protected by shoveled moats
of flowing water.
Sand in the car
and passing around treats
from grandma's brimming cookie jar.
The smell of lilacs
wafting all the way home
from Spokane to Seattle.

Fabric of Worry

Aboard the ferry
she threads a needle—
    eye shifting open wide to slit of consternation.
Single snag interrupts smooth repair of unexpected rupture.

Grandbaby is happy without its mommy until mommy reappears.
Oh, the wailing at shock of recognition who's been missing.

Mother holds slender metal between thumb and forefinger
    while her son rides his motorcycle
    homeward along the coast highway.
        She winces at not knowing

        whether basting beforehand helped,
        reassures herself luck comes to some—
        always triple knots edge of her mending.
        Blind stitches can't hide in tough fabric.
Large-eyed needles could alternate as search engine—
        thread effect to match each fabric color
though some won't notice emergency repair
of lilac floral, blue denim, black leather, rainbow fleece.

Keys, diplomas. pacifiers, tangle up in thread, all those rows
        of commonplace repetition.
        Mother hears warning on the ferry
to check seams before re-inserting children into carry-on bags, and
utilizes narrow steel well-forged, rubbed smooth to reduce resistance
        between warp and weft—
    as if the carbon steel's shiny nickel
    would mend, connect, adhere one worry to another
    allow multi-tasking.
    SAFETY FIRST!
But thimbles are often afterthought. And each unwary pin prick bleeds.

Prism

Riddles read ribbons and strawberries wrinkle
Old onions cry out once pumpkin seeds twinkle
Yolks of eggs become sunshine with daffodils laughing
Grass garlic peas leaves on trees gently grasping
Bright sky sweet pea robin's egg forget-me-nots
Ink indigo eggplant inside wild welcome-me-thoughts
Vast lilacs, king 'n queen royals in velvet spring rain
Richard of York Gave Battle In Vain

The Poet's Coffin

let the grief-stricken
peruse library shelves to select
          one memento mori—gather

to toast the poet
in simile
and extended metaphor—gather

and layer remaining books on carpet
in tightly woven frame
during dusk to dawn wake—gather

first edition hardbacks
with biodegradable glue to form
a cadaver-sized container—gather

paperbacks full of penciled marginalia
to cushion said poet's eternal inside
discard all tucked away files—gather

first drafts or letters of rejection
slant layers of loose poems in poet's
favorite font before inserting sinewy body—gather

papyrus fibers to shroud
surround poet's face and hands with bundles
of abundant fresh lilacs—gather

said poet's own letters of acceptance
scroll and tie with ribbon to tuck
as if a crown of juxtaposed syllables—gather

penny nails to tap semantic casket shut
while lightly scented mourners
chiding end-stopped lives continue to—gather

Blue Poem

Blue day:	Intermittently morose but I still am connecting
Blue night:	Surprising what a little indigo will do
Blue day:	I am at the door of sadness
	I hurt feelings when the low-grade pressure washer
	plies grout between my neighbor's pavers
	Persistence gains a bad name when
	the picnic moves inside
	Sixty-decibel drone in ninety-degree heat
	Eat the sound of dead lilacs
Blue night:	Blackberries are darker than blueberries
	Hard bumps vs. firm circle
	Their taste is so much harder to come by
	Blackberries depend upon thorns
	Vines are frequently nonproductive
Blue day:	There remains the edge of sadness
Blue night:	Is the edge removable?
Blue day:	More like a tinge over the luster
Blue night:	Yes, I recall
Blue day:	Are we from the same ten acres not ever planted?
Blue night:	Perhaps of a volunteer species?
Blue day:	Sometimes birds dribbled on my roots after nibbling
	Seeds scattered without prevarication
Blue night:	We are tastier in turmoil
Blue day:	I've always envied indigo
Blue night:	It's a thunder and lightning world
Blue day:	I'm afraid of the night sky
Blue night:	Your flowers are gorgeous but don't bear fruit
	Okay as they blossom blue bell, blue lilac,
	lobelia, forget-me-not
Blue day:	Blackberries clinging to vinegar on broiled salmon
	If only pungent inspiration could be so constant
Blue night:	I will add gentian, iris, butterfly ash shadows
Blue day:	Garden sky in my big blue eyes

Saving Lilacs

Spent blossoms
        continue
                to radiate
                        lilac aldehyde
                                Petals
                        shrivel
                their curved
        foursomes
Green sprigs
        drooping
                Green leaves
                        sparkle shine
                                from waterfall
                        on woody branches
                beside a porch
        beside a door
You offer all
        that is left
                to bring inside
                        bring inside
                                me

Since you ask how do we love a sibling (enough)

What   Happens when our father balks
Can't afford, but   Education is the ticket insists mom
Four paper routes   Lilac City's news mom & sisters help
Jim carries also   In sling bag hopes pro-football jersey
At least until   X-Ray shows NY Giant body damage

No more we   Hold coal from a chute in our hands
Next generation   Escapes steam and diesel engines
Never   Long for a job during the Depression
Dad's legacy   Inherits family tremor from the old sod
Train derailment   X-ray showed his shaking's sudden onset

          Heavenly Father, honest but inebriation
          Envelops the brain with consequence
          Luck of the Irish fits the stereotype
          I stoke fire of monogrammed baby rattles
          X-rated angst delivered to his children:

Clean 'n sober   Her glamour, oldest Katherine buries two
St. Patrick's Day   Educator Fredene's heart stops in church
Pushing daisies, we Lose Jim's heart on his Universal Gym
Sort it out   I'm last child of Fred and Ethel's DNA
In therapy   X-ray history with time's gray photos

Remember, give   Homage to what remains
One thought   Each other was the lucky one
No use dwelling on Leaves ripped from the climbing tree
Two of us left   In distant states, oldest & youngest
The 50s jukebox   XOXO football & A&W root beer floats

Lost and Found

In the movie of my life
Vermeer's pearl earring girl
would be pulling threads
from the bottom of a tapestry
to repair midnight shadows
stitch back ochre leaf veins
olive green foot paths
lilac worn threads
dun paw of a dog
lavender tufts nuzzled by bees
all inadvertently ripped
in those years of hanging
beside a stone staircase.

CPSIA information can be obtained
at www.ICGtesting.com
Printed in the USA
JSHW031237231020
8964JS00002B/144

9 781646 623174